I See a Pr

What's the Problem?

Manuel Martinez

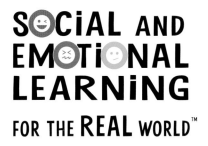

S😀CiAL AND
EM😣Ti😑NAL
LEARNiNG
FOR THE **REAL** WORLD™

You have a problem.
How can you fix it?
What's the first step?

The first step to fixing any problem is to see the problem.
Then, you can make a plan!

Imagine you did poorly
on a math test.
Ask yourself a question.
What's the problem?

Your problem may be that you didn't understand the work. Now, make a plan!

You can talk to your teacher.
They can help you learn
from your mistakes.

Imagine you had a fight
with your brother.
What's the problem?

Your problem may be that
your brother took your tablet.
What can you do?

You can talk it out
with your brother.
Tell him how you feel.

Fixing a problem isn't always easy. Sometimes you need to look at it a new way.

Figure out your problem
and think about it.
Then, you can start to fix it!

Words to Know

brother

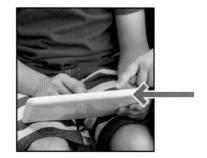

tablet

teacher